Kit and Dog

Written by Jeanne Willis
Illustrated by Sarah Horne

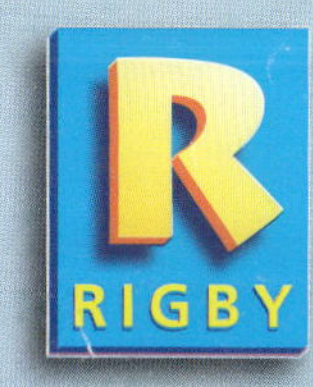

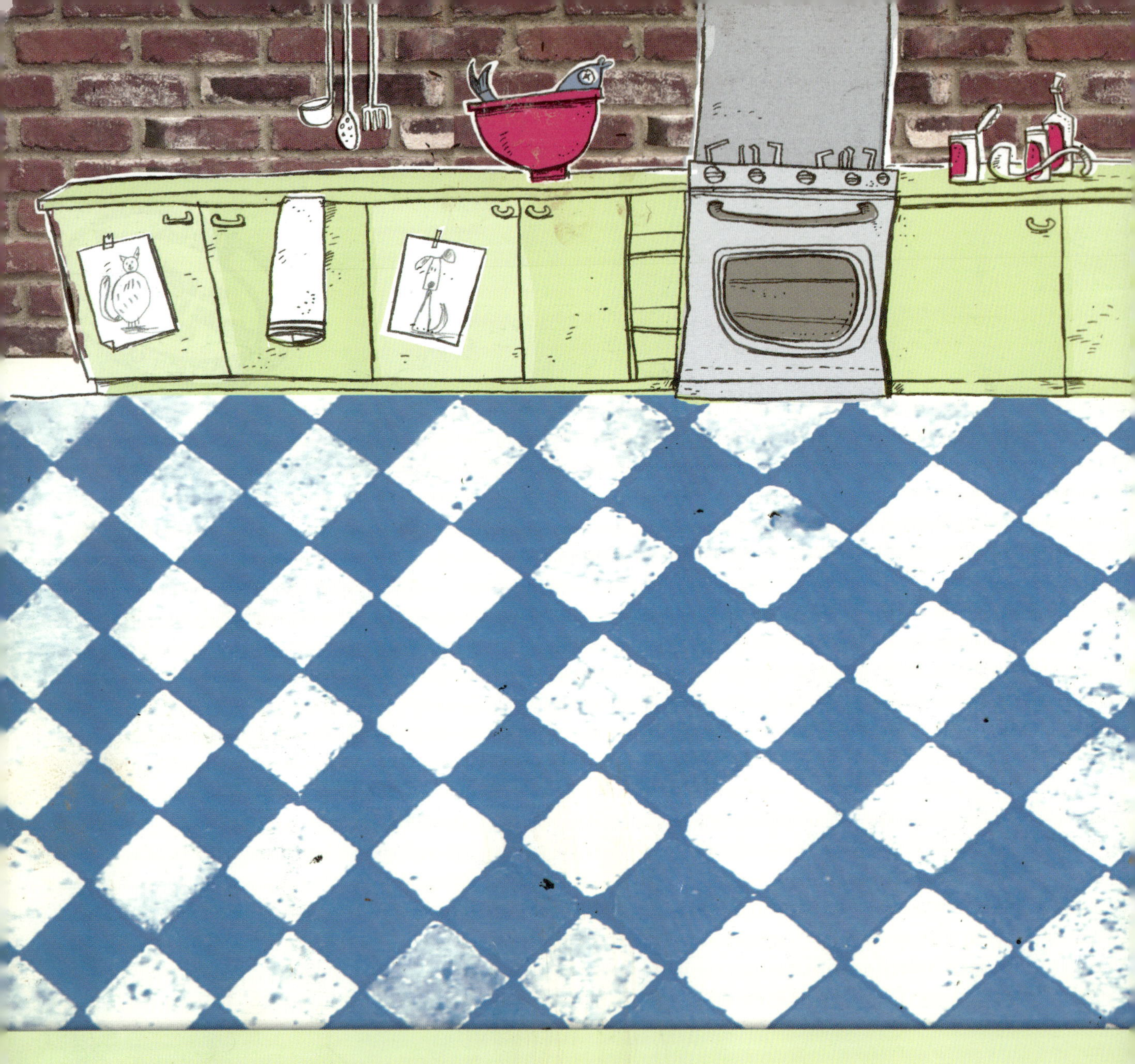

A cod in a pot.

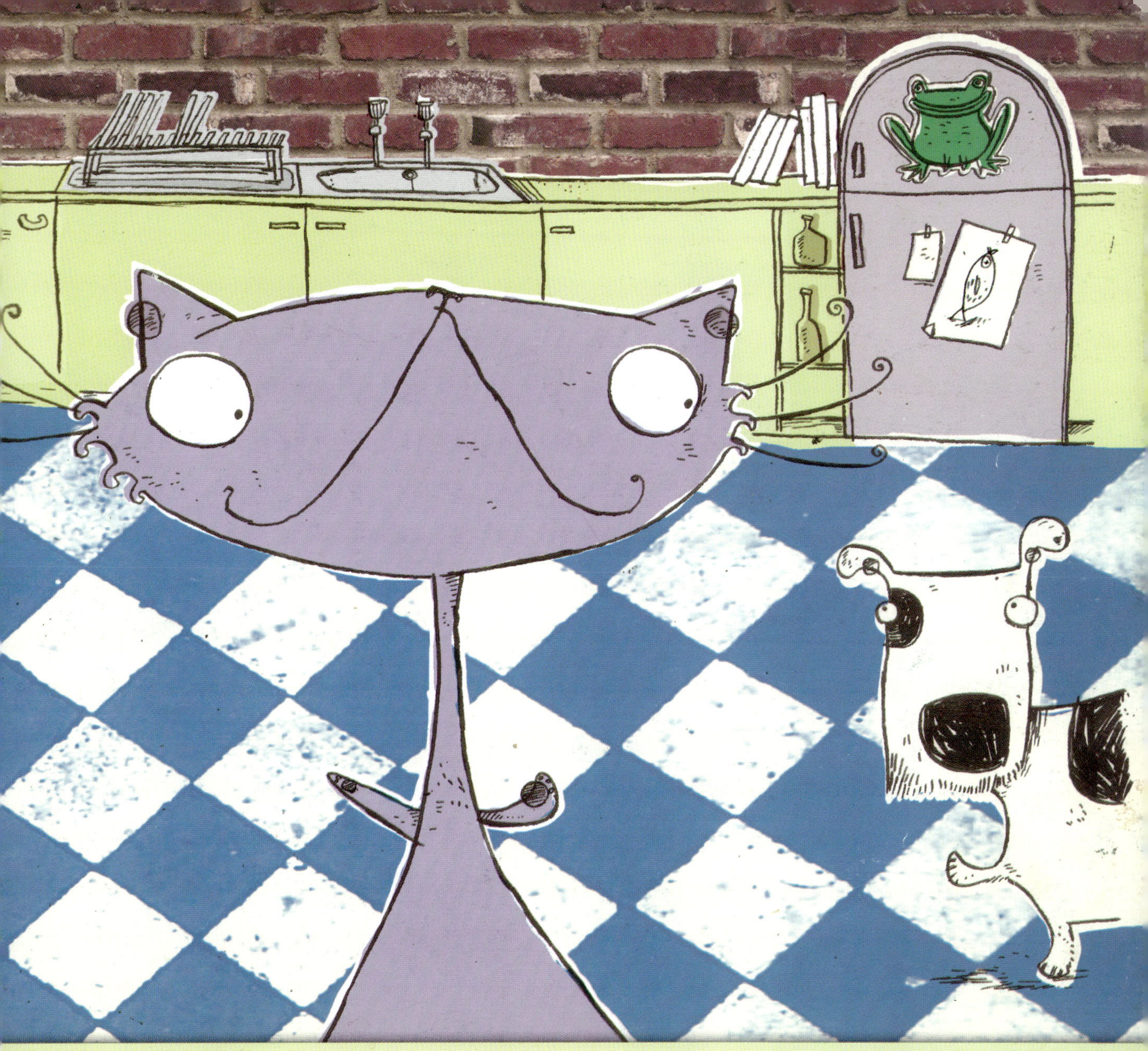

Kit got Dog.

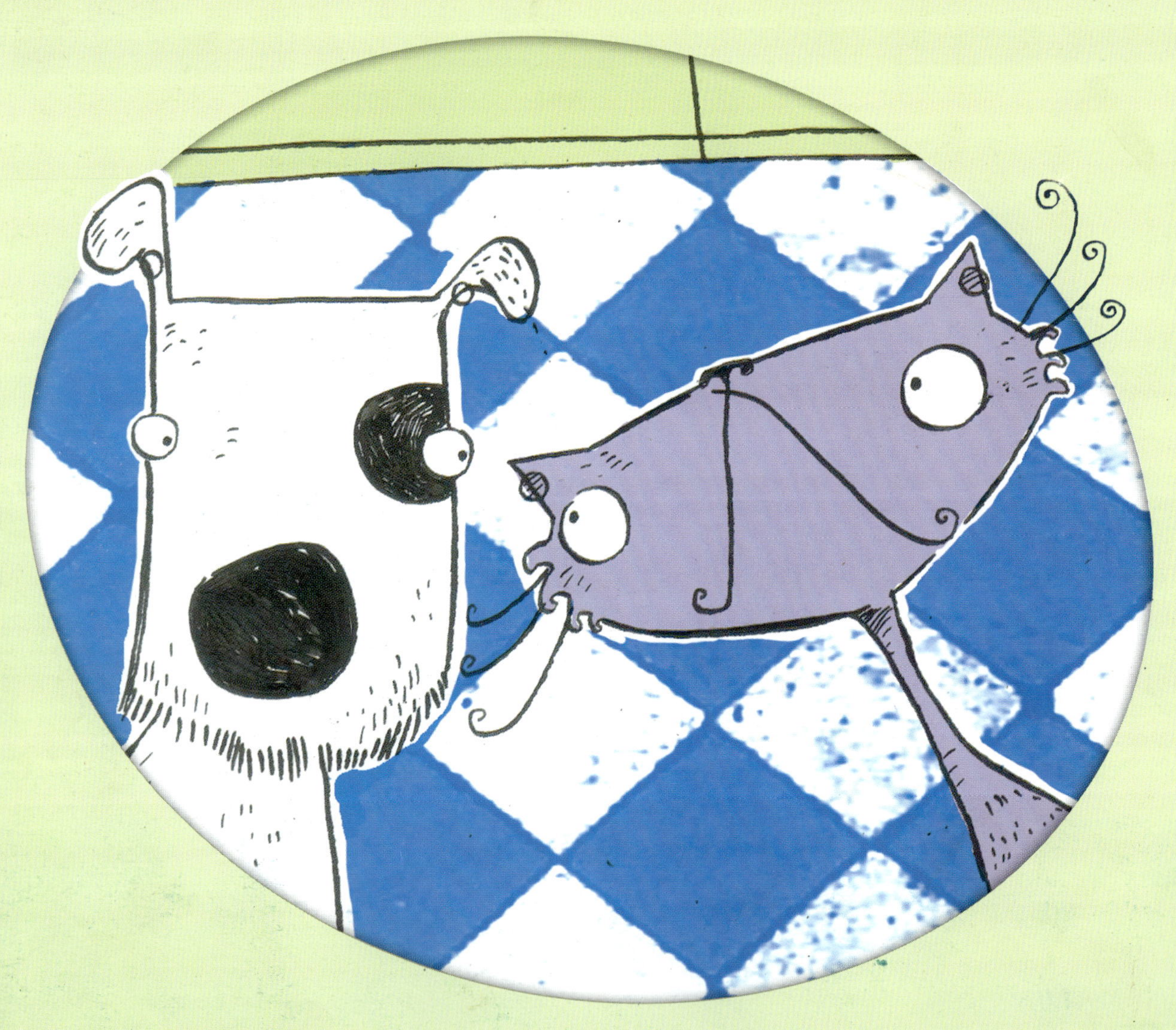

Dog nods to Kit.

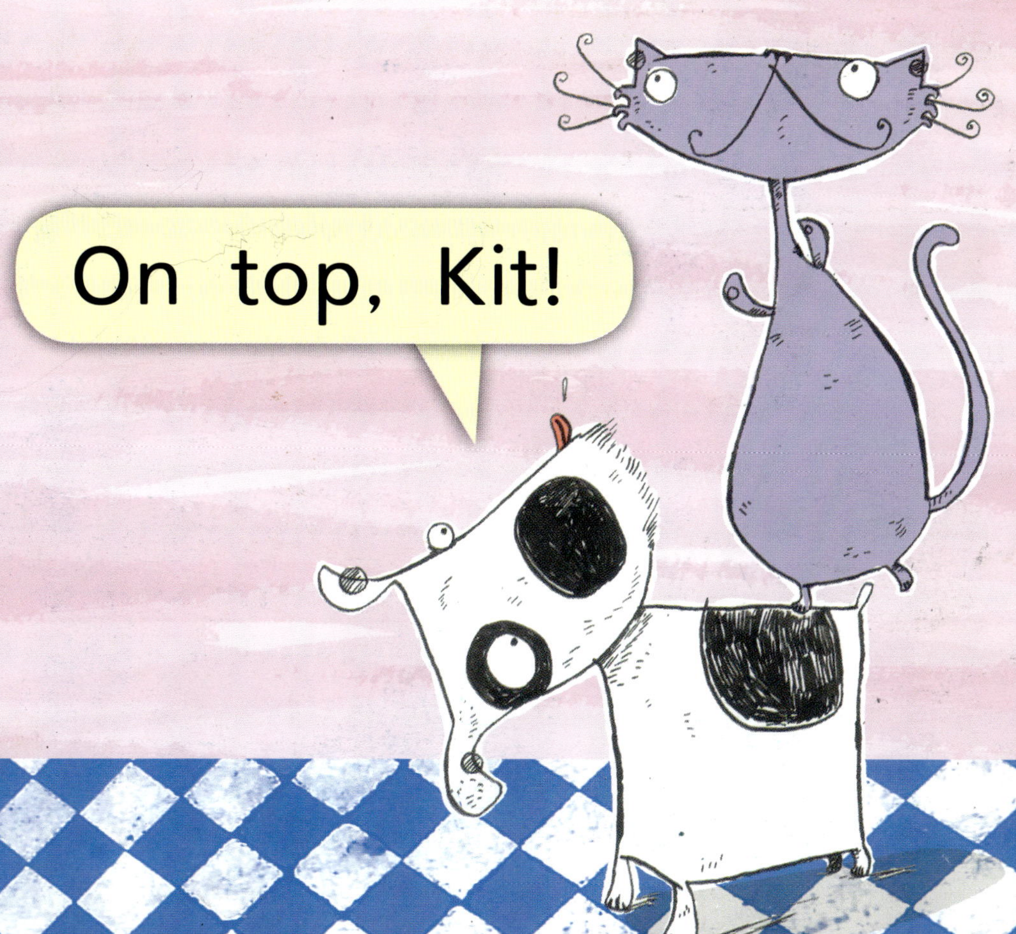
On top, Kit!

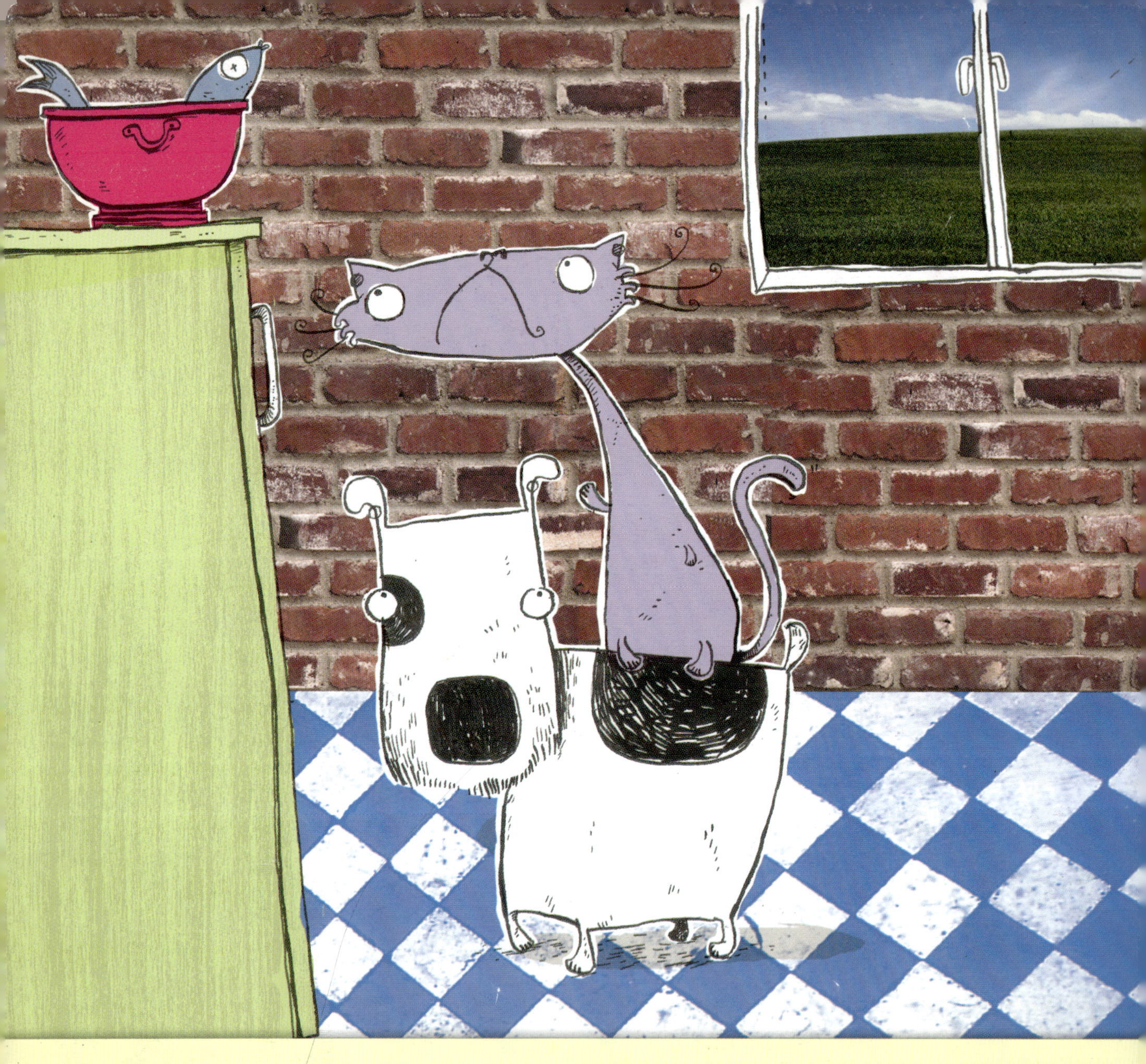

Kit is on Dog.

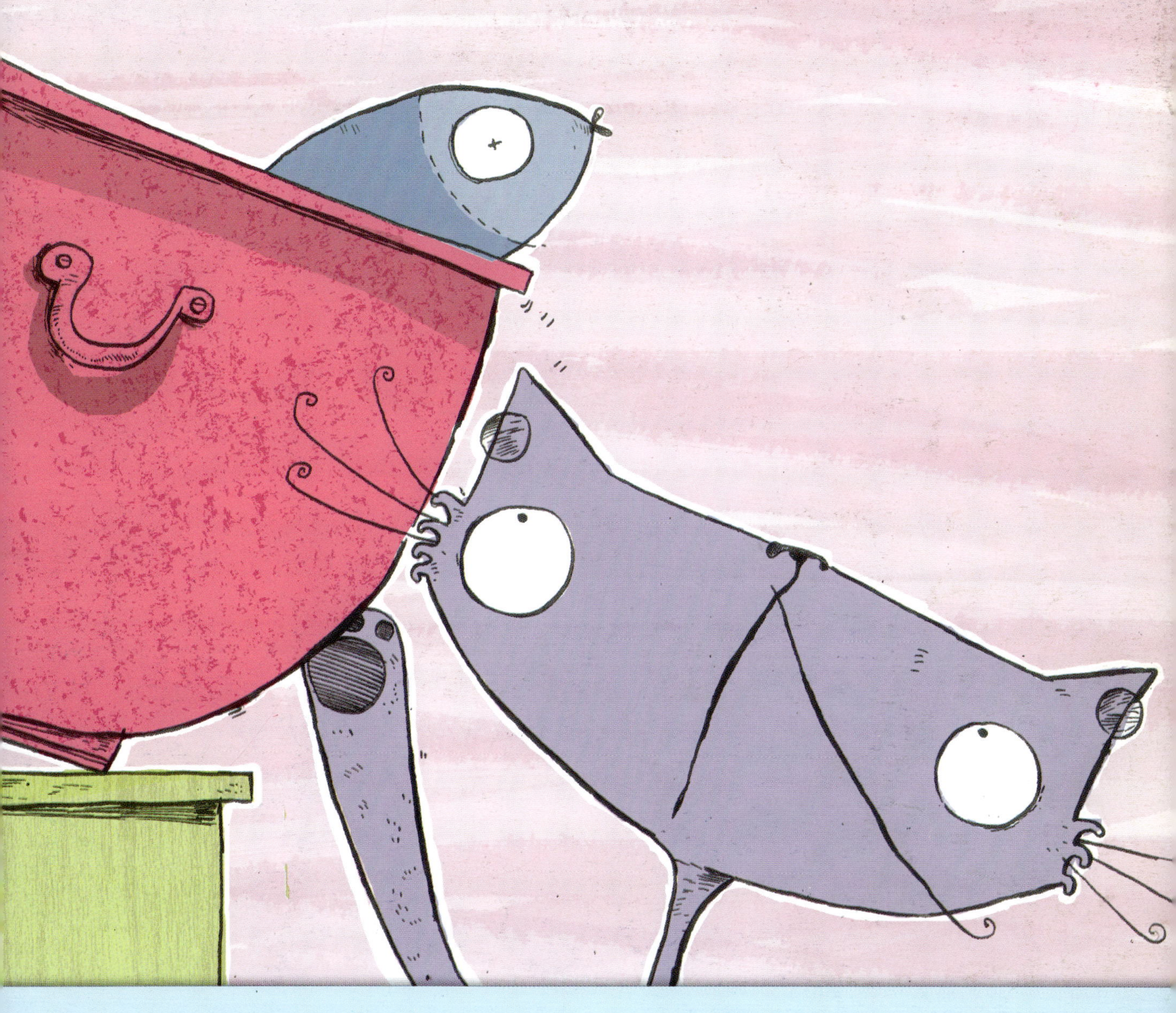

Tip, tip, tip ...

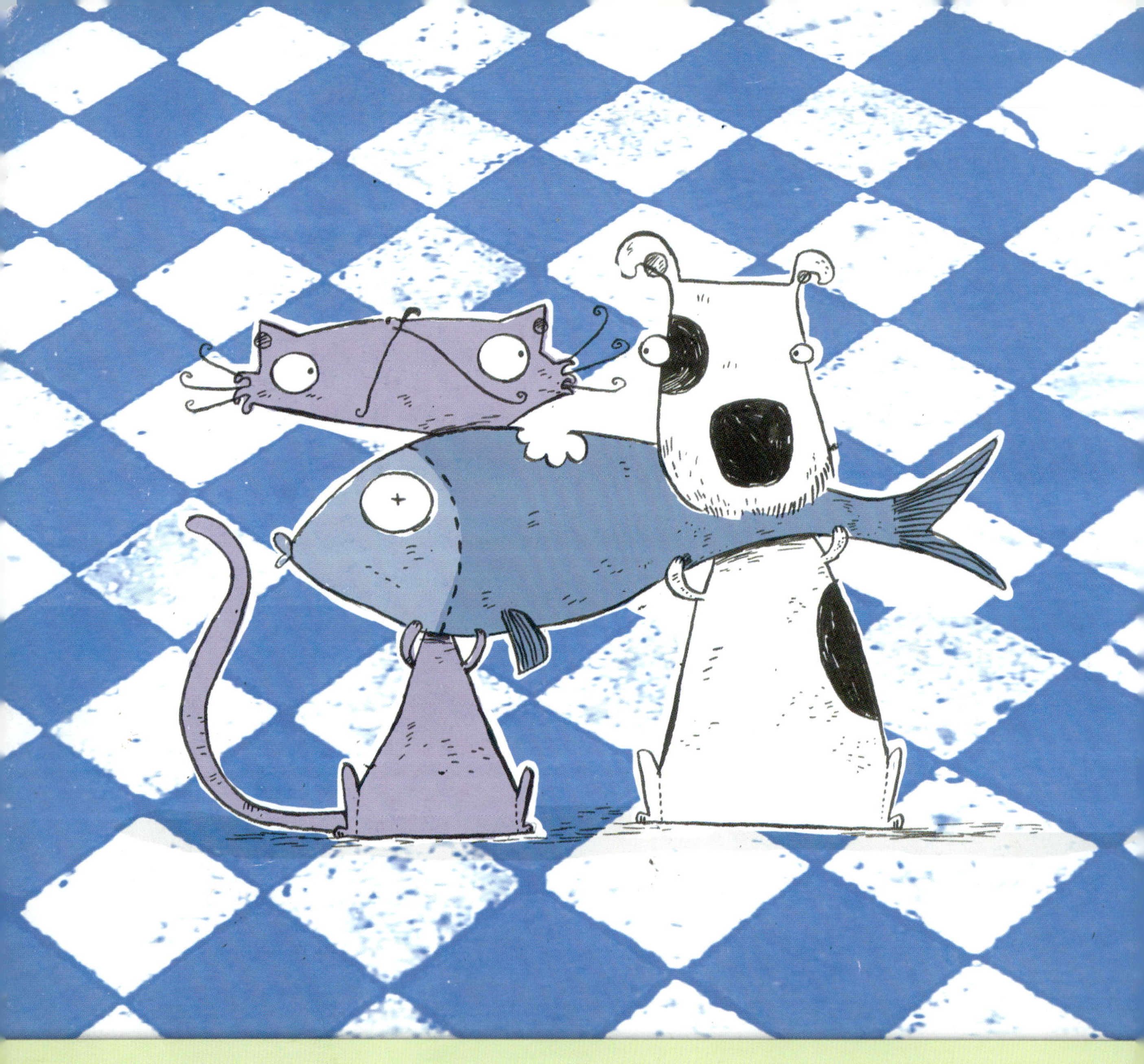

Kit and Dog got a cod!